T0062292

Building a Gaming PC

21st Century Skills **INNOVATION LIBRARY**

Josh Gregory

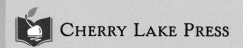
CHERRY LAKE PRESS

Published in the United States of America by Cherry Lake Publishing Group
Ann Arbor, Michigan
www.cherrylakepublishing.com

Reading Adviser: Beth Walker Gambro, MS, Ed., Reading Consultant, Yorkville, IL

Photo Credits: ©Syafiq Adnan / Shutterstock, cover, 1; ©I2pTink3r / Shutterstock, 5, 10; ©Stanisic Vladimir / Shutterstock, 8; ©george photo cm / Shutterstock, 13; ©stockphoto-graf / Shutterstock, 14; ©grafvision / Shutterstock, 16; ©Grigvovan / Shutterstock, 19; ©WildSnap / Shutterstock, 21; ©THANAN KONGDOUNG / Shutterstock, 22; ©Patrik Slezak / Shutterstock, 23, 28; ©EKKAPHAN CHIMPALEE / Shutterstock, 25; ©Tanawat Thipmontha / Shutterstock, 27; ©socrates471 / Shutterstock, 29; ©DC Studio / Shutterstock, 31

Library of Congress Cataloging-in-Publication Data

Names: Gregory, Josh, author.
Title: Building a gaming PC / by Josh Gregory.
Description: Ann Arbor, Michigan : Cherry Lake Publishing, [2022] | Series:
  21st century skills innovation library | Includes bibliographical
  references and index. | Audience: Grades 4-6
Identifiers: LCCN 2021042744 (print) | LCCN 2021042745 (ebook) | ISBN
  9781534199651 (library binding) | ISBN 9781668900796 (paperback) | ISBN
  9781668902233 (ebook) | ISBN 9781668906552 (pdf)
Subjects: LCSH: Microcomputers—Design and construction—Juvenile
  literature. | Computer games—Juvenile literature
Classification: LCC TK7886 .G74 2022 (print) | LCC TK7886 (ebook) | DDC
  621.39/16—dc23
LC record available at https://lccn.loc.gov/2021042744
LC ebook record available at https://lccn.loc.gov/2021042745

Cherry Lake Publishing Group would like to acknowledge the work of the Partnership for 21st Century Learning, a Network of Battelle for Kids. Please visit http://www.battelleforkids.org/networks/p21 for more information.

Printed in the United States of America
Corporate Graphics

Josh Gregory is the author of more than 125 books for kids. He has written about everything from animals to technology to history. A graduate of the University of Missouri–Columbia, he currently lives in Chicago, Illinois.

Contents

CHAPTER 1

Piece By Piece

If you're a serious video game player, you've probably thought about building your own gaming PC. Building a custom machine allows you to play games exactly how you want to. For some people, that means pushing technology to the limits and enjoying high-end three-dimensional (3D) graphics at a very fast **frame rate**. For others, it means creating the perfect setup to enjoy classic games of decades past. Some players might even build a custom PC perfectly designed for a single game!

Every PC building project should begin with plenty of research. Even the most experienced builders go online to do some reading and watching before they start working on a fresh machine. There are always new technological advances to learn about, new features to try, and new games to play. Keeping up to date with all of this information is part of the fun of the hobby. You'll want to check out reviews of different PC parts and see what kinds of machines other players are putting together.

If you've never built a PC before, you'll have a lot to learn about computer **hardware** and the ways different parts work together. The number of possible combinations of parts you can use to put together a PC is nearly limitless. However, there are a few major types of parts you'll need to include in every build.

A brand-new, empty PC case is like a blank canvas. You get to decide every detail of what goes inside!

Don't Break the Bank

A new gaming PC can be a big investment. If you want a machine that can play the latest games, you'll likely need to spend at least a few hundred dollars. A machine with the latest, most powerful parts can cost thousands! The important thing is to figure out how much you have to spend before you start picking out parts. Then stay within your budget! If you want to splurge on a fancy video card, you might need to buy a cheaper motherboard. Or maybe you can shop around to find great deals on the parts you want. Try not to stretch your budget to its limit, either. You might realize later that you need some money to buy things like a keyboard and mouse!

First, you'll need a case to hold all of the other parts. Most modern PC cases are shaped like rectangular boxes. However, there are all kinds of different ones, from tiny boxes designed to sit under your TV like a video game console to cases meant to be mounted on a wall. For beginners, it's usually best to stick to a standard size and shape. This will make it easier to pick out parts that fit and assemble them safely.

Next comes the motherboard. This is a big circuit board full of different slots and connectors. The motherboard will be mounted inside of the case. All the other parts will then plug into the motherboard.

This means the size and shape of your case will determine which motherboard you can use. And the motherboard you use will determine which other parts you can use.

The **processor**, or central processing unit (CPU), is the main "brain" of the computer. It is usually a small chip that fits into a slot on the motherboard. A CPU can generate a lot of heat when it is running. To keep it from overheating, a large fan system or other cooling device gets installed on top of it.

Sticks of random access **memory** (RAM) will also slot directly into the motherboard. When you run a program, your computer loads files into the memory. The more RAM you have, the more complex games your machine can run.

A hard drive is necessary to store files on your computer. Bigger hard drives will allow you to install more games at once. Some kinds of hard drives are also much faster than others. When it comes to gaming, a faster hard drive means shorter loading times. If your hard drive is fast enough, you might barely need to wait around at all when you load up a game.

A typical gaming video card has its own cooling system with two or three fans.

It might not be the most exciting piece of your PC, but a good power supply is essential. This device takes power from the electrical outlet in your wall and sends it out to all the different parts of your PC. Some power supplies can provide more electricity than others. Make sure you pick one that can comfortably power your machine.

While you don't need a video card to get a computer up and running, you DO need one to run most modern games. A good video card can really make the difference when it comes to high-end graphics. If that's important to you, aim for the most advanced card that fits your budget.

If you have all of the things listed above, you have everything you need to build a gaming PC. There are all kinds of other optional parts you can include in your build. You'll probably also want a monitor, a mouse, and other devices to make your computer more functional. But the first step is just getting a working PC put together!

Feeling familiar with the main parts of a PC? The next step is to decide what kind of machine you want to build. Every PC gamer has different goals in mind. First, ask yourself which games you want to play. Then investigate what kinds of system **specs** are recommended for those games. You should also consider whether you will want to use your PC for things other than playing games. For example, do you want to edit videos or record music? You might need some special gear to do those things well.

Next, try to figure out a list of parts that will come together to make your idea a reality. You need to make sure all of the parts are **compatible** with each other. One way to do this is to start with one part you know you want. For example, let's say you already have a video card in mind. Next, look for a motherboard that supports your chosen video card. Then figure out what kinds of CPUs and RAM the motherboard

Try to gather all the parts you need before you start building. Don't start opening packages until you're ready to put everything together.

supports. Can you come up with a good combination that meets your needs?

Try to avoid bottlenecks as you pick your parts. A bottleneck is when you put a very powerful part in a PC where the other parts are not quite as powerful. The rest of your PC could hold the powerful part back from reaching its full potential, much like the narrow neck of a bottle holds liquid back from flowing out all at once. This won't make your PC explode or anything like that. It is a big waste of money, though. For example, one mistake some beginners make is pairing a top of the line video card with a slower CPU. The PC can still work just fine, but the same results could have been achieved with a cheaper video card.

Finally, you'll need an **operating system** for your computer. This is the **software** that allows everything to work. For a gaming PC, you will pretty much always want to use the latest version of Microsoft Windows. Windows will give you access to the widest variety of games, and it is compatible with most gaming devices.

CHAPTER 2

Some Assembly Required

Once you have all the parts you need, it's time for the fun part—putting everything together. If you've never built a PC before, it might look like it's going to be complicated. But don't worry. In the end, it isn't too much different from putting together a LEGO set or a model kit!

Before you start, there are a few things you should do to get ready. First, clear aside a good amount of space on a table or countertop. If you can, avoid locations where you have to stand on carpet. Make sure the work surface is clean, and get all of your PC parts together nearby. Don't open any of the boxes yet.

Next, make sure you have tools nearby. You probably won't need much more than a screwdriver and a variety of bits. Most of the parts will be able to snap together without tools, but you'll at least need to screw the motherboard into the case.

Remember than electricity can be dangerous. You should never work on a computer that is turned on or plugged in. The good news is that there's no risk at all if the computer is unplugged. In fact, there is actually more risk of static electricity from your body damaging a piece of hardware! To avoid this, don't stand on carpet as you work. It also helps to wear shoes with a

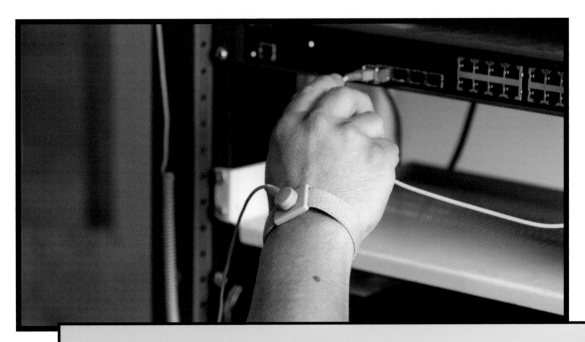

Professionals often wear bracelets like this when working with electronics. The wire can be clipped onto any piece of metal to prevent you from transferring static electricity from your body to a computer part.

A new motherboard will look something like this when you take it out of its packaging. However, the different ports are not always arranged in the same way.

rubber sole. If you are really concerned, you can buy a special bracelet that wraps around your wrist and clips on to your PC case to prevent any static from traveling from your hands to your PC parts.

Once you're ready, start by opening up the package for your motherboard. There should be an instruction manual inside. Keep this handy as you work, and be sure to save it when you're done. It will almost always contain a diagram showing what each and every slot and connector on your motherboard is for. The box for your motherboard might also contain some cables and other small parts. Set these aside for now.

The motherboard itself will be wrapped in a special anti-static plastic. Each of your parts will come in a similar wrapper. As you work, it is good to set parts on top of these wrappers instead of putting them directly on the table. Handle your motherboard carefully as you remove it from its wrapper. Then set it down flat on your work surface.

A Helping Hand

If you've never built a PC or worked with electricity before, it really helps to have someone with more knowledge nearby to offer help and advice. Ask a parent, older sibling, or another trusted adult if they will give you a hand. Try to do as much on your own as you can. But don't be afraid to speak up if you aren't sure about something. After all, you don't want to ruin an expensive piece of PC hardware. The important thing is to learn as you go. Next time you put a PC together, it will be a breeze!

Next, open up your CPU. Read the instructions that come with it, as well as the instructions for your motherboard. This should show you how to install the CPU. Be very careful as you set the CPU on the motherboard. Do not force anything into place. Once the CPU is installed, set the motherboard aside. Don't install the CPU cooler yet.

Next, open up your case. Take a good look at how it goes together, and read any instruction manuals that

A CPU socket looks like this. Be very careful to avoid damaging any of the tiny pieces of metal sticking up from the motherboard.

come with it. Your case will usually come with a variety of screws, brackets, and other pieces. Set them aside for now. Your next goal is to mount the motherboard in the case. The screw holes on the motherboard should match up with the ones inside the case, and it should only fit together one way. Refer back to the instruction manuals if anything is confusing.

Once the motherboard is mounted in the case, connect the case's internal wires to the motherboard. For example, there will be a wire running from the case's power button, and others from any lights or ports on the front of the case.

Next, install the power supply in the case. There is usually only one way for the power supply to fit. Some power supplies will have a bunch of wires permanently attached. Others have plugs for you to attach only the wires you want to use. Either way, these wires will connect the power supply to the other parts inside your PC. There will be one large wire that plugs into a large port on the motherboard. Then there will be a bunch of smaller ones that lead to everything from your video card to hard drives and any fans inside your case. Exactly which wires you need will depend on what kinds of parts are inside your machine. As always, refer back to your instruction manuals as needed.

Now is a good time to install your CPU cooler. This device can be large and bulky, so installing it any earlier might leave you with less room to work. Once it's in place, you can slot in your sticks of RAM. Check the diagram in your motherboard manual to see which slots they go in.

Next, install your hard drives. Some kinds plug into your motherboard directly, much like RAM or a CPU. Others will be mounted in the case and attached to the motherboard using a cable. Different cases have different ways of mounting hard drives. Usually, there is a piece that needs to be screwed onto the hard drive. Then that piece attaches somewhere inside the case.

The final piece to install is your video card. The video card in a gaming PC is usually fairly large, so it's good to save it for last. There will be a slot on the motherboard for the card to slot into, much like a stick of RAM. Usually, you will also need to tighten a screw to hold the back of the card steady on the case. Finally, the video card will need to be connected to the power supply.

Most cases will have a setup something like this for installing traditional hard drives.

Congratulations! You've done most of the work of assembling a PC. But even though all the main parts are put together, you're not quite done yet.

CHAPTER 3

Finishing Touches

It's usually not a great idea to try booting up your PC right off the bat as soon as the main parts are assembled. Instead, do a final check to make sure everything is plugged in correctly. Make sure wires are connected the ways you see in the instruction manuals. Also, make sure everything is plugged in all the way. Loose connections are a common problem for PC builders at all levels of experience. And even one loose wire can keep your PC from booting up, so it's worth double-checking.

Once everything is in place, take a close look at your case. Make sure to remove any spare wires, screws, or other bits and pieces. Many cases also feature brackets and other pieces that can be removed if they aren't needed. It can be helpful to remove these extra pieces to make it easier to access the inside of the PC for repairs later on. However, be sure to set them aside. They might come in handy if you add any new parts to your machine!

Next, you should take a moment to double-check the positioning of the different fans in your case. Most cases have many possible locations to mount fans. You will want at least two of them: one that sucks air in, and another that pushes air out. Ideally, these should be on opposite sides of the case. This allows the PC to

Most modern cases include a large number of spots where you can install fans, but you don't need to use all of them.

pull in cool air and spit out the warm air. It's a good idea to install more fans if you have a powerful PC. More powerful hardware tends to produce more heat. If you do, follow the same basic rules of a two-fan setup. The idea is to create a cool breeze that passes through the inside of your computer.

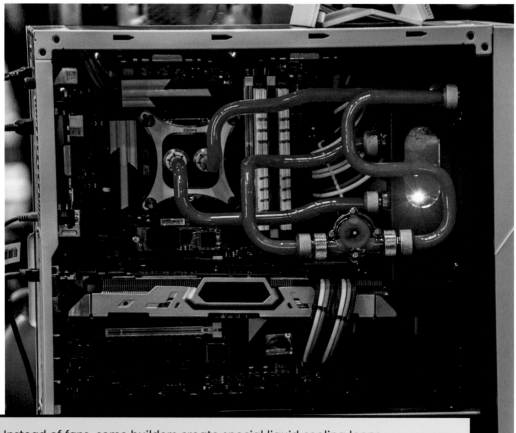

Instead of fans, some builders create special liquid cooling loops. These are much quieter than fans, but putting one together takes a lot of work. It's not a good choice for beginners!

Most cases allow you to stash wires and cables behind the place where your motherboard is mounted. This keeps them out of sight from the other side of the computer.

Another worthwhile thing to do is clean up all of the various wires connected inside the case. You can use wire ties or similar tools to bundle them together and keep them out of the way. Be sure to keep them away from fans. Many modern cases also have built-in hooks and other pieces inside to help you keep your wires organized. The more wires you leave hanging around, the more places dust can gather.

Your PC might get hotter, and it will definitely be more of a pain to put in new parts or take out old ones.

Once you've double-checked everything and cleaned up the inside of the case, go ahead and close the case up. Hopefully, you've already decided on a spot to put your PC. A good location should have some space on all sides of the case so air can flow through. You should

Getting Creative

Some PC gamers get very creative with their cases. They might put colored lights inside or paint the outside in bright colors. Some expert builders even create their own custom cases from scratch. They post pictures online and compete to create the wildest designs. You might see PC cases in the shape of Star Wars characters, or a PC built inside the outer case of a retro video game console. You definitely don't want to try anything like this with your first PC. But eventually, it might be something you can try for yourself!

also avoid setting your PC on carpet or a rug. A hard floor is OK, or you can set the PC on top of a desk. Place your PC where you want it, then get out your monitor, keyboard, and mouse. Now it's time to plug everything in and see if your PC works.

Most PC gamers have all kinds of accessories, from game controllers to headsets.

CHAPTER 4

Booting Up

When you press the power button for the first time, hopefully your PC will boot up without any trouble. But every PC builder has run into a situation where things don't go as planned. Don't worry. You just need to do a little troubleshooting.

First, check once again to make sure that everything is plugged in where it is supposed to be, and that all connections are secure. You'd be surprised how often the problem is something as simple as a stick of RAM that isn't securely plugged into the motherboard.

If you still can't get your PC to start up, you might have a bad piece of hardware. Motherboards, RAM, and other important pieces can sometimes be faulty or damaged before you ever take them out of the box. It's not something you should expect all the time, but it does happen. So how do you determine which part is causing trouble? Unfortunately, this can be time-consuming. The most reliable way to figure it out is to go through your new PC and replace each part one by one with a spare part you are sure works. The biggest problem for a first-time builder is that you need spare parts handy for this to work.

Faulty RAM is a common problem when building a new PC. However, there is no way to tell if a stick of RAM is bad until you try to use it.

You can also try to do some detective work to figure out what the problem is. Take the side panel off of your computer if it doesn't have a window. When you flip the power switch, do the fans start spinning? Do you see any light or hear any beeps from your motherboard? If nothing happens at all, you probably have a problem with your power supply or something isn't plugged in

If you're having trouble booting your new PC, the first thing you should do is make sure the power cable is plugged in and the power supply is switched on.

Some computers don't just have a window on the side; they are completely clear!

correctly. If it seems like your PC is running, but you aren't seeing anything on the screen, there might be an issue with the video card. Try to think carefully about what is and isn't working. Consider what each part of the PC does. This will help you figure out where the problem lies.

If you do have a faulty part, send it back for a working replacement. Most stores and manufacturers deal with these situations quickly and easily. They know it happens from time to time, and they should be happy to help.

Once your machine is up and running, go back and look through all the packaging from your PC parts. Set aside all the manuals and any extra pieces that came with the parts. You might need them later on. If you have room, it can also be good to keep the boxes the parts came in. This will make it easier to trade or sell them later on if you decide to **upgrade**.

Looking Ahead

No matter how good your PC is, it will one day be out of date. But you don't need to build a whole new computer when you want a boost. Once you have a PC, you can upgrade individual parts one at a time. For example, you could swap out your video card for a new one and keep everything else. Or you could keep your old case and power supply, but swap out the rest of the parts. As long as the parts are compatible, you can combine new ones together however you like.

Even if you're having fun building and tinkering, don't forget to actually test your PC out with some games once in a while!

Now comes the best part: playing games! Building your first PC is just the beginning. It could be the start of a lifelong hobby. There is always more to learn and discover. But for now, just have fun!

GLOSSARY

compatible (kuhm-PAT-i-buhl) able to work together

frame rate (FRAYM RAYT) a measurement of how many times per second the image on screen changes when playing a game

hardware (HARD-wair) the physical parts that make up a computer

memory (MEM-uh-ree) a device that is able to hold information for later use

operating system (AH-pur-ay-ting SIS-tuhm) a program, such as Microsoft Windows or macOS, that controls the functions of a computer

processor (PRAH-sess-ur) the central "brain" of a computer that processes information

software (SAWFT-wair) computer programs

specs (SPEKS) details of a computer's abilities

upgrade (UP-grayd) to replace something with a better version

FIND OUT MORE

Books

Cunningham, Kevin. *Video Game Designer*. Ann Arbor, MI: Cherry Lake Publishing, 2016.

Loh-Hagan, Virginia. *Video Games*. Ann Arbor, MI: Cherry Lake Publishing, 2021.

Powell, Marie. *Asking Questions About Video Games*. Ann Arbor, MI: Cherry Lake Publishing, 2016.

Websites

Logical Increments
www.logicalincrements.com/
This incredibly useful website will help you find parts that work well together and see how much they cost.

PC Gamer: 2021 Gaming PC Build Guide
www.pcgamer.com/gaming-pc-build-guide/
Check out some PC part recommendations from one of the biggest PC gaming magazines.

INDEX